Threee:
Three One-Act Plays

Colleen Neuman

A SAMUEL FRENCH ACTING EDITION

SAMUEL FRENCH
FOUNDED 1830

SAMUELFRENCH.COM
SAMUELFRENCH-LONDON.CO.UK

Copyright © 2009 by Colleen Neuman
All Rights Reserved
Graphic Design by Gene Sweeney

THREEE is fully protected under the copyright laws of the United States of America, the British Commonwealth, including Canada, and all other countries of the Copyright Union. All rights, including professional and amateur stage productions, recitation, lecturing, public reading, motion picture, radio broadcasting, television and the rights of translation into foreign languages are strictly reserved.

ISBN 978-0-87440-214-8

www.SamuelFrench.com
www.SamuelFrench-London.co.uk

FOR PRODUCTION ENQUIRIES

UNITED STATES AND CANADA
Info@SamuelFrench.com
1-866-598-8449

UNITED KINGDOM AND EUROPE
Theatre@SamuelFrench-London.co.uk
020-7255-4302

Each title is subject to availability from Samuel French, depending upon country of performance. Please be aware that *THREEE* may not be licensed by Samuel French in your territory. Professional and amateur producers should contact the nearest Samuel French office or licensing partner to verify availability.

CAUTION: Professional and amateur producers are hereby warned that *THREEE* is subject to a licensing fee. Publication of this play(s) does not imply availability for performance. Both amateurs and professionals considering a production are strongly advised to apply to Samuel French before starting rehearsals, advertising, or booking a theatre. A licensing fee must be paid whether the title(s) is presented for charity or gain and whether or not admission is charged. Professional/Stock licensing fees are quoted upon application to Samuel French.

No one shall make any changes in this title(s) for the purpose of production. No part of this book may be reproduced, stored in a retrieval system, or transmitted in any form, by any means, now known or yet to be invented, including mechanical, electronic, photocopying, recording, videotaping, or otherwise, without the prior written permission of the publisher. No one shall upload this title(s), or part of this title(s), to any social media websites.

For all enquiries regarding motion picture, television, and other media rights, please contact Samuel French.

MUSIC USE NOTE

Licensees are solely responsible for obtaining formal written permission from copyright owners to use copyrighted music in the performance of this play and are strongly cautioned to do so. If no such permission is obtained by the licensee, then the licensee must use only original music that the licensee owns and controls. Licensees are solely responsible and liable for all music clearances and shall indemnify the copyright owners of the play(s) and their licensing agent, Samuel French, against any costs, expenses, losses and liabilities arising from the use of music by licensees. Please contact the appropriate music licensing authority in your territory for the rights to any incidental music.

IMPORTANT BILLING AND CREDIT REQUIREMENTS

If you have obtained performance rights to this title, please refer to your licensing agreement for important billing and credit requirements.

THE LION WHO ROARED

CHARACTERS

LION
GIRAFFE
ZEBRA
LEOPARD
ANTELOPE
ELEPHANT
OSTRICH
PYTHON
RHINOCEROS
PARROTS 1, 2, 3, 4, 5

MONKEYS 1, 2, 3, 4
ANT
SPIDER
BEETLE
OLD BABOON
ARMADILLO
ARMADILLO CHILDREN 1, 2, 3, 4
TOUCAN
GAZELLE
HYENAS 1, 2

A NOTE ON CASTING

The play is written for a cast of 31. It may be performed by a larger or smaller cast by adjusting the number of PARROTS, MONKEYS, ARMADILLO CHILDREN and HYENAS.

Doubling is not possible since the whole cast is on stage throughout the play.

None of the roles are gender specific.

COSTUMES

Black t-shirts, black pants, black socks and colored baseball caps with character-appropriate ears attached. For example, **LEOPARD** will wear a black or gold baseball cap and the ears will be gold with black spots.

PROPS

Small suitcase
Rope that looks like a vine
Throat spray

SET

One stool
Jungle trees, shrubs and flowers, as desired

(All the characters except **LION** *are scattered around at center and right.* **HYENAS** *are standing back to back, leaning against each other, arms folded.* **MONKEYS** *are sitting in a jumble, legs and arms tangled together.* **ARMADILLO** *sits at center, her children curled in balls in a close circle around her, heads on each other's backs.* **PARROTS** *sit in a straight line facing audience, shoulder to shoulder, heads all tipped in the same direction and resting on their neighbor's shoulder.* **ANT, SPIDER** *and* **BEETLE** *lie on their sides in a line, heads resting on neighbor's feet. The individual animals –* **TOUCAN, OSTRICH, GAZELLE, PYTHON, ELEPHANT, GIRAFFE, ZEBRA, ANTELOPE** *and* **LEOPARD** *– each sit or stand or lie alone, here and there around the groups, each in a different position.* **OLD BABOON** *sits on a stool, a little apart and to the right. All the animals are asleep, heads bowed forward or tilted to the side, eyes closed.)*

*(***LION***, offstage left, roars. Animals start to wake up a little.* **LION** *roars again. Animals wake up a little more.* **LION** *roars a tremendous roar. Animals are now all awake and not very happy about it.)*

GIRAFFE. *(waking up, stretching, still very tired)* Are you awake, Zebra?

ZEBRA. *(reluctantly raising head, opening eyes)* No. In order to be awake I would have to be first asleep. So first I was not asleep and now I am not awake. So I am neither.

GIRAFFE. Did you sleep, Leopard?

LEOPARD. Not a spot. I was up all night listening to…

*(***LION** *roars.)*

ANTELOPE. As was I.

ELEPHANT. And I.

OSTRICH. And I.

PYTHON. And me.

RHINOCEROS. And me.

PARROTS 1, 2, 3, 4, 5. And we.

HYENAS 1, 2. *(pointing to each other)* And he.

MONKEYS 1, 2, 3, 4. *(pointing to* **ANT**, **SPIDER**, **BEETLE***)* And they.

ANT, SPIDER, BEETLE. *(pointing to* **MONKEYS***.)* And them.

GIRAFFE. Ssssshhhhh. Old Baboon sleeps.

OLD BABOON. *(opens eyes)* I do not sleep, Giraffe. I rest my eyes. It is what Old Baboons do.

(closes eyes)

ARMADILLO. *(awake and packing a small suitcase)* And I was up all the jungle night long listening to…

*(***LION** *roars.)*

And listening to my children cry…

*(***ARMADILLO CHILDREN** *huddle close to* **ARMADILLO** *and cry.)*

When they hear…

*(***LION** *roars.* **ARMADILLO CHILDREN** *huddle closer, cry harder.)*

So I am packing.

PYTHON. *(shocked)* You wouldn't leave, Mrs. Armadillo?

ARMADILLO. I wouldn't stay! Not when I can move to the mountains where, I am told, lions have manners. They roar at the sun and purr at the moon and everyone…

(a long, dreamy sigh as she says this)

Sleeeeeeeeeeeeps.

ALL. *(echoing* **ARMADILLO***'s long, dreamy sigh)* Aaaaaaaaahh-hhhhhh.

GIRAFFE. *(Going to* **ARMADILLO***. Very nervous.)* But aren't you afraid? Mountains, I am told, are high. You could fall off.

ARMADILLO. Better to fall off ten mountains, Giraffe, than lie awake one more night because…

(LION roars. ARMADILLO CHILDREN crowd closer to her and cry.)

Of that. Come, children.

(One child takes hold of the back waistband of ARMADILLO's pants. All the children take hold of the back waistband of the pants of the child in front of them.)

Hold tight!

(Exits right with CHILDREN trailing behind her.)

OSTRICH. *(stunned)* A corner of the jungle with no Mrs. Armadillo.

RHINOCEROS. And no Armadillo Children.

(sadly shaking head)

What a shame.

ANT. *(sadly shaking head)* What a shame

SPIDER. *(sadly shaking head)* What a shame.

BEETLE. *(sadly shaking head)*What a shame

ALL. *(sadly shaking heads)* What a shame, shame, shame, shame, shame.

MONKEY 1. And all because our corner of the jungle has this lion who...

(LION roars.)

MONKEY 2. All the jungle day long and...

(LION roars.)

MONKEY 3. All the jungle night long and...

(LION roars.)

MONKEY 4. In all the times between day and night. Which makes life most difficult.

TOUCAN. Why, it was just last Tuesday that the Gorillas left...

GAZELLE. And the Hippopotamus left the Thursday before that with my friend the Egret riding on his back. I miss him.

(Those close to her pat her on the back.)

PARROT 1. And we are the only five Parrots left.

PARROT 2. Our mothers and fathers and brothers and sisters…

PARROT 3. And thousands of cousins…

PARROT 4. Have flown to South America and vowed never to come back to this corner of the jungle.

PARROT 5. We miss them.

(**PARROTS** *pat each other on the back.*)

MONKEYS 1, 2, 3, 4. And now this.

(Sadly shaking heads.)

HYENA 1. (**HYENAS** *don't see what all the fuss is about.*) There are still two hyenas.

HYENA 2. And that is all that matters.

PARROT 1. *(Disgusted. To other* **PARROTS**.*)* Which is what the hyenas always say.

(**PARROTS** *shake heads in disgust.*)

ANTELOPE. *(Has been thinking hard during all of this and startles himself by having an idea. A step or two forward.)* Something must be…

(struggling to say a new and unfamiliar word)

Done.

ELEPHANT. What do you mean?

ANTELOPE. Somebody must…

(stuggles to get it out)

Do something.

LEOPARD. I have never heard of such a thing! We are jungle animals. There is no 'doing' in the jungle. We do not 'do.' We eat, we sleep…

ANTELOPE. *(going to* **LEOPARD**) But we don't sleep! And if we don't 'do' something, every animal will be an Armadillo finding a mountain to move to.

(going to **ZEBRA**)

You and I, Zebra – we, too, will go.

ZEBRA. *(incensed)* Never! Zebra has lived here as long as Lion. Why should bad manners send good manners packing off to the tops of mountains?

GIRAFFE. *(very frightened)* Perhaps to fall off and be smashed to bits.

ZEBRA. A giraffe shouldn't be afraid of heights.

GIRAFFE. But is.

LEOPARD. *(going to* **OLD BABOON***)* Old Baboon, what do you think of this 'doing?'

OLD BABOON. *(opens eyes)* I think you must either 'go'…

(gestures right where **ARMADILLO** *exited)*

Or 'do.'

(gestures left to **LION***.* **LION** *roars.* **OLD BABOON** *closes eyes)*

ANTELOPE. Ah! We must either 'go'…

(gestures right)

Or 'do'.

(Gestures left. **LION** *roars.)*

ALL. Hmmmmmmmmmmm.

LEOPARD. I don't want to go…

MONKEY 1. Nor I.

PARROT 4. Nor I.

MONKEY 3. Nor me.

PARROT 3. *(pointing to* **MONKEY 4***)* Nor he.

MONKEY 4. *(pointing to* **PARROT 3***)* Nor she.

PARROTS 1, 2, 5. *(pointing to each other)* Nor we.

ALL. Nor any of the all of us.

LEOPARD. So how do we do this 'do?'

ELEPHANT. *(pushing herself forward, very self-important)* I have a proposal!

ANT. *(very weary of* **ELEPHANT***)* Elephant always has a proposal.

SPIDER. Her mother was the same before her.

BEETLE. And all of her children after her.

ELEPHANT. *(annoyed by their comments, even more self-important)* I propose that we go to Lion and talk.

GIRAFFE. Does Lion use his teeth when he talks?

LEOPARD. Lion uses his teeth when he does everything.

GIRAFFE. He will eat us, one by one.

ELEPHANT. Ah, but we will not go one by one. We will go in a...

(very important word)

De-le-ga-tion. I will lead the Delegation. Who will follow?

LEOPARD. *(joining* **ELEPHANT** *with more resignation than enthusiasm)* Me, I suppose. I am his cousin so he might bite me a little but he won't eat me.

ZEBRA. *(joining* **ELEPHANT** *and* **LEOPARD***)* And Zebra! I don't care a stripe for his teeth!

PYTHON. Zebra is sometimes inspired.

OSTRICH. And sometimes stupid.

ANTELOPE. *(joining* **ELEPHANT**, **LEOPARD** *and* **ZEBRA***)* And I, Antelope. Because this is 'doing' something. I think.

HYENA 1. (**HYENAS** *pushing in rudely as they join* **ELEPHANT**, **LEOPARD**, **ZEBRA** *and* **ANTELOPE**.*)* And we will go...

HYENA 2. Because there may be something in it for *us*.

RHINOCEROS. Which is what the hyenas always say.

ANTELOPE. And you, Giraffe?

GIRAFFE. *(backing away a few steps)* But lions eat meat and I am made of meat. And so are you all.

ELEPHANT. Ah! The lion eats meat but he does not eat Delegations. Probably.

ANTELOPE. And you, Old Baboon?

OLD BABOON. *(opens eyes)* Old Baboons do not go or do. Old Baboons rest their eyes.

(closes eyes)

I will be here.

MONKEY 4. Old Baboon is always here…

MONKEY 5. And will be always here.

PYTHON. *(addressing the* **DELEGATION***)* We, the animals remaining behind, wish you luck for talking.

GAZELLE. And, if your luck is bad, speed for running…

OSTRICH. A tall tree for climbing…

RHINOCEROS. And a rock for hiding behind!

TOUCAN. And while you are gone, we will . . ?

GIRAFFE. Hide!

(A general scurry as they hide here and there, in little groups, behind each other, cover faces with hands, crouching down to floor. The **DELEGATION** *forms a line with* **ELEPHANT** *at the left end of it.)*

ELEPHANT. *(leads* **DELEGATION** *as they snake around the stage and the huddles of animals, gradually getting further left)* And I, Elephant, lead you, the Delegation, this way…

ANTELOPE. And that way…

ZEBRA. And in and out and in…

HYENAS. And through…

LEOPARD. And around and over and under our corner of the jungle…

*(***LION** *roars.* **DELEGATION** *comes to abrupt halt.)*

ELEPHANT. *(frightened)* We are very close!

(runs to the other end of the line, cowers there)

LEOPARD. I thought you were going to lead.

ELEPHANT. First I led at the front. Now I will lead at the back.

ANTELOPE. *(now at the left end of the line and, by default, the leader)* Come along…

(starts to lead them left)

HYENA 1. *(***HYENAS** *refusing to move.)* We aren't going any further.

LEOPARD. But you are part of the Delegation.

HYENA 2. We are hyenas and you can't make us do anything we don't want to do.

*(**LION** roars an especially nasty roar.)*

HYENAS. *(Running away back to the other animals. Cower there.)* Aaaaaaaahhhhhhhh!

ANT. *(Disgusted with **HYENAS**.)* And the hyenas will spend the rest of the day cheating at cards.

SPIDER. Which is what hyenas always do.

BEETLE. It is what makes them hyenas.

*(**LION** has stalked on and struck an impressive pose left. **DELEGATION** is looking after the **HYENAS** and hasn't noticed **LION**.)*

ANTELOPE. *(starting to lead **DELEGATION** left)* I think we are almost there…

*(Bumps into **LION**. **LION** roars.)*

We are there!

LION. Ah, it is you, Lowly Antelope. Have you come to worship me?

ANTELOPE. *(**DELEGATION** is very meek and timid in the presence of **LION**.)* I have. We all have…

LEOPARD. Sire…

ZEBRA. Sir…

ELEPHANT. Your Sire-ness.

LION. You may worship me now.

(strikes a pose)

ANTELOPE. *(**DELEGATION** is in a scared huddle.)* Oh, we already do…

LEOPARD. We never stop worshipping you.

ZEBRA. Worshipping you is our greatest pleasure.

*(**ELEPHANT** says nothing. **ZEBRA** gives **ELEPHANT** a nudge. **ELEPHANT** nods and squeaks.)*

*(strutting around them, enjoying being **LION**)* And that is as it should be. I am, after all, Lion. God of animals. Biggest, strongest…

(roars)

Loudest.

ANTELOPE. And we admire you for it.

(LEOPARD, ZEBRA and ELEPHANT nod enthusiastically.)

And we, the lowly animals who are nothing but dust under your great and mighty paws . .

LION. *(admiring his paws)* They are great and mighty, aren't they? I love my paws. Everything about me is great and mighty. I love everything about me. Especially my teeth.

(shows teeth to ELEPHANT)

Don't you?

(ELEPHANT nods and squeaks.)

ANTELOPE. And we have a favor to ask that only your great and mighty Lion self can grant.

LION. *(a yawn)* Ask.

(ANTELOPE clears throat nervously. LEOPARD, ZEBRA and ELEPHANT push ANTELOPE a little forward, encouraging her.)

ANTELOPE. Perhaps your great and mighty roaring, which is such a pleasure all the jungle day long...

(LEOPARD, ZEBRA and ELEPHANT nodding their agreement.)

Perhaps it could be a little less great and mighty during the jungle night so we, the lowly animals, can get our pathetic and meaningless sleep?

LION. *(not happy)* What?

ANTELOPE. Could you be just a little...

(big gulp)

Quieter?

(ANTELOPE, LEOPARD, ZEBRA and ELEPHANT brace themselves.)

LION. *(pretending to consider it)* Ah. Quieter? Quiet roaring.

(ANTELOPE, LEOPARD, ZEBRA and ELEPHANT starting to look relieved.)

How does one roar quietly?

ANTELOPE. *(whispering)* Roar?

LION. *(stops pretending)* That is how an antelope roars. This is how Lion roars!

(Huge roar!)

It is what makes me Lion. Everyone wants to be Lion but only I can do it.

LEOPARD. *(a careful step closer to **LION**, appealing to reason)* Come along now, Lion. Cat to cat, I have bags under my eyes for not sleeping. And I believe my spots are fading from fatigue.

LION. *(circles **LEOPARD** in disgust)* Leopard, you are a pathetic sort of cat, aren't you? Spots. The right kind of cat doesn't need spots. I have no spots. You're lucky they're fading. When they're gone completely, you will look more like me.

ANTELOPE. But…

LION. But my teeth remind me I eat meat.

*(going nose-to-nose with **ANTELOPE**)*

And you are made of meat, aren't you, Antelope?

ANTELOPE. *(quaking with fear)* I am.

LION. *(nose-to-nose with **LEOPARD**)* And Leopard?

LEOPARD. *(shivering with fear)* Yes.

LION. *(nose-to-nose with **ZEBRA**)* And Zebra?

ZEBRA. *(cowering with fear)* Uh-huh.

LION. And Elephant?

*(**ELEPHANT.** is paralyzed with fear. Squeaks.)*

LION. So you will go away now and not bother me and my teeth again about all this roaring nonsense or my teeth will get itchy and I will have to scratch them with your bones.

*(A menacing roar. **DELEGATION** is hurriedly backing away, bowing, stumbling.)*

ANTELOPE. It is our pleasure to obey you…

LEOPARD. It honors us to obey you…

ELEPHANT. All animals in the jungle worship and honor and obey you…

ZEBRA. Except the Popalopalus who says you are nothing.

> (**DELEGATION** *freezes in horror, including* **ZEBRA** *who is astounded that such a thing came out of her mouth.*)

LION. *(a cold, mean narrowing of eyes)* The who?

ZEBRA. *(Can't get out of it now. Tries to be casual as she tells lie after lie.)* Why, the Popalopalus. The new animal. Haven't you met him?

LION. I have not had the pleasure. And he lives where in my jungle?

ZEBRA. He lives everywhere and nowhere. Or so he says.

LION. What else does he say?

ZEBRA. Oh, just that he is bigger and stronger and so on and so forth than any animal in the jungle and that lions are nothing.

LION. *(increasingly annoyed)* Does he?

ZEBRA. Oh yes. He says he would be lion. But it bores him.

LION. Does it? Bores him, does it? Well, we shall see. We shall see about boring your…

> *(can't remember the name)*

ZEBRA. Popalopalus.

LION. Bring your Popalop…?

> *(still can't remember it)*

ZEBRA. *(helping him)* Alus…

LION. Here and we shall see how bored he is when I am done with him!

ZEBRA. Oh, he won't come.

LION. *(unheard of)* Won't come?! I command it!

ZEBRA. He doesn't take commands.

LION. *(enjoying this)* He is afraid!

ZEBRA. Oh no. He isn't afraid of anything. He won't come anywhere without there being a contest. Contests are the only places he goes so he can prove he is biggest…

LION. I am biggest!

ZEBRA. Strongest…

LION. I am strongest!

ZEBRA. Loudest.

LION. *(can't believe his ears)* Loudest? He says he is louder than Lion? Louder than my…

(The loudest roar so far.)

ZEBRA. He laughs at your roar.

LION. *(grabs* **ZEBRA** *by the collar)* You, Zebra, you will find this…?

(Still can't quite remember the name.)

ZEBRA & LION. (**ZEBRA** *starts out and* **LION** *joins in about half-way through.)* Popalopalus.

LION. You will bring him here. And you will tell him there will be contests. I go now for my morning drink. See to it that he is here when I return.

(stalking off left)

ANTELOPE. Yes, your Mightiness.

LEOPARD. Yes, your Greatness.

*(***ELEPHANT** *squeaks.)*

*(***LEOPARD, ANTELOPE** *and* **ELEPHANT** *crowd excitedly around* **ZEBRA** *when* **LION** *is safely gone.)*

LEOPARD. This is wonderful! Such news! A new animal! And you didn't tell us!

ANTELOPE. Where did you meet him?

ELEPHANT. Where is he from?

ZEBRA. *(Looking increasingly fearful. Runs back to other animals.)* Aaaaaaaahhhhh!

*(***ANTELOPE, LEOPARD** *and* **ELEPHANT** *hurry after her.)*

MONKEY 3. They are back!

(All the animals come out of hiding.)

MONKEY 2. The Delegation has returned!

(All the animals crowd around the returning **DELEGATION.***)*

GIRAFFE. *(examining* **LEOPARD**'s *arm)* And no teeth marks! It went well then?

LEOPARD. Beyond our wildest dreams! There is a new animal in the jungle!

ANTELOPE. An animal who thinks Lions are nothing!

ELEPHANT. An animal who will be in a contest with our Lion!

ALL. *(thrilled)* Aaaaaaaahhhhhh!

LEOPARD. Only Zebra has met him!

ANTELOPE. *(Going to* **ZEBRA** *who is looking more and more upset.)* Tell us, Zebra – where did you meet him?

ELEPHANT. Where is he from?

GIRAFFE. What does he eat?

*(***ZEBRA** *sinks to knees, bursts into tears.)*

TOUCAN. Why are you crying?

PYTHON. The excitement has been too much for her.

GAZELLE. She needs a nap.

ELEPHANT. *(back to being self-important)* Being part of a Delegation is tiring work.

ZEBRA. There is no new animal!

(weeps copiously)

LEOPARD. Of course there is! And his name is Popalopalus!

ALL. *(very exciting)* Aaaaaaaahhhhhh! Popalopalus!

ZEBRA. There is no Popalopalus! I made him up!

(And more weeping. The other animals are horrified.)

LEOPARD. You what?!

ANTELOPE. You made him…

(can hardly bear to say it)

Up?!

ELEPHANT. He is a…fiction?!

*(***ZEBRA** *nods.* **ELEPHANT** *squeaks.)*

LEOPARD. Are you mad? What caused you to say this thing?

ZEBRA. *(awash in regrets)* I was inspired!

(weeps)

ALL. Or stupid!

SPIDER. Your inspiration will be the death of us all!

ANT. We shall all be eaten!

BEETLE. What inspiration will there be in that?

ZEBRA. None!

(weeps)

MONKEY 1. When Lion finds out its all lies…

MONKEY 2. He won't like it.

MONKEY 3. No, he won't.

MONKEY 4. The only lies he allows are his own.

ZEBRA. *(Stops weeping. Has an idea.)* Unless…

PYTHON. Oh no!

ZEBRA. We could…

RHINOCEROS. Don't listen!

ZEBRA. Build one!

ALL. *(hands over ears)* We can't hear you!

ZEBRA. *(jumping to his feet)* We will build a Popalopalus!

LEOPARD. *(horrified)* This is more inspiration!

OSTRICH. Or stupidity.

GAZELLE. One doesn't build an animal.

OSTRICH. Animals are complicated.

ZEBRA. *(grabs OSTRICH, chooses a spot, makes OSTRICH kneel on spot, very erect, arms straight down at sides)* You are a leg!

OSTRICH. *(offended, trying to get up)* I am an Ostrich!

ZEBRA. *(pushing OSTRICH back into place)* You are an Ostrich pretending to be a leg.

(Grabs RHINOCEROS, chooses another spot, makes him kneel and puts him in the same pose.)

And you are a leg!

RHINOCEROS. *(having none of it, getting up)* I am a Rhinoceros!

ZEBRA. *(pushes RHINOCEROS back into place)* You are a Rhinoceros pretending to be a leg.

PYTHON. *(Understands what* **ZEBRA** *is doing. Chooses the correct spot to be another "leg," kneels and assumes the pose.)* And I am a Python pretending to be a leg!

ZEBRA. Yes!

GAZELLE. *(putting herself in place)* A Gazelle can be a leg as well as a Python!

*(***LION*** *roars a mighty roar from off left.)*

ANTELOPE. Hurry! I hear him coming!

*(***ZEBRA*** *hurriedly arranging more animals into a large group that will be the "torso" to which the "legs" are connected.* **ZEBRA** *bends each one straight forward at the waist. They are close to each other – shoulder to shoulder, hip to hip.)*

ZEBRA. And you are the middle!

*(***LION*** *roars.)*

LEOPARD. He is getting closer!

ZEBRA. *(putting* **GIRAFFE** *where the "head" will be)* And you are the front!

GIRAFFE. *(very afraid)* Not me!

ZEBRA. *(no time to argue)* Yes, you!

*(***LION*** *roars.)*

ELEPHANT. And closer!

(squeak)

ARMADILLO. *(hurrying on from right with her children, all still hanging on to each other)* I heard there is a new animal! We hurried back as fast as we could…

ZEBRA. *(placing* **ARMADILLO** *and* **ARMADILLO CHILDREN** *at back to be the tail)* You are the tail!

ARMADILLO. *(offended)* I am an Armadillo!

ALL. You are the tail!

*(***LION*** *roars.* **ARMADILLO** *and* **ARMADILLO CHILDREN** *become the tail without further discussion.)*

LEOPARD, ANTELOPE, ELEPHANT. And closer!

TOUCAN. And the rest of us?

ZEBRA. *(frantic)* Hide!

(The animals who aren't part of the **POPALOPALUS** *scramble around, find a spot, curl up, hide faces. All the animals who are part of the* **POPALOPALUS** *bow their heads low to hide their faces as* **ELEPHANT, ANTELOPE, LEOPARD** *and* **ZEBRA** *get ready to greet* **LION.***)*

LION. *(enters left, roaring)* I am here!

*(***ELEPHANT.** *squeaks.)*

I waited for you. I do not like waiting. So I came to find you. I followed the smell of meat.

ZEBRA. We apologize for our rudeness but the Popalopalus prefers it here.

LION. *(eyeing the* **POPALOPALUS,** *not impressed)* So this is him then?

ZEBRA. Oh yes – where are my manners? Mister Popalopalus, it is my pleasure to present, His Greatness, His Mightiness – Lion.

LION. *(Waits to be greeted as royalty. There is only silence. Insulted.)* He does not speak?

ZEBRA. Of course he speaks!

(A hard nudge to **GIRAFFE** *who reluctantly looks up.)*

GIRAFFE. *(high, squeaky voice)* Hello! I mean…

(lowers voice very low)

Hello.

LION. *(circling* **POPALOPALUS***)* I have never seen such an animal.

LEOPARD. If you had seen such an animal, he wouldn't be new.

LION. *(eyeball to eyeball with* **GIRAFFE***)* I, Lion, challenge you, Popalopalus, to one, two, three contests – biggest, strongest, loudest!

(roars)

ZEBRA. And, Old Baboon, you will be judge?

LION. We do not need a judge. I will win.

OLD BABOON. *(opens eyes)* Lion, your bluster does not frighten me. I am too old to care about teeth. If there is no judge, there is no contest. There is only showing off. I will be judge.

LION. It does not matter – judge or no judge. I will win.

OLD BABOON. The first contest will be: who is biggest?

LION. I tower over him as I tower over you as I tower over everyone...

ZEBRA. *(pointing with false excitement behind **LION**)* Oh look! Over there!

LION. *(turns and looks)* What?

*(**ZEBRA** quickly makes the "legs" stand up. As they do, **ANTELOPE**, **LEOPARD** and **ELEPHANT** go to **LION** and continue the distraction.)*

LEOPARD. Oh yes! There!

*(pointing in a different direction as **ZEBRA** quickly makes "torso" unbend)*

ANTELOPE. Astounding!

*(Pointing in a different direction as **ZEBRA** makes the animals an arm's length away from each other with hands resting on neighbors' shoulders, backs and so on so they're still connected.)*

ELEPHANT. Amazing!

*(Pointing in a different direction as **ZEBRA** has "tail" stretch as far back as possible, until the last **ARMADILLO CHILD** is actually offstage right but still holding on to the child in front of her, and has all the animals in the **POPALOPALUS** raise their heads so their faces are no longer hidden.)*

LION. *(looking from one direction to the next, seeing nothing)* What?! Where?!

ANTELOPE. *(seeing **POPALOPALUS** is ready)* Oh, it's gone.

LION. What was it?

LEOPARD. If you do not know what it was, Your Greatness, how could we?

LION. *(accepting the compliment)* True.

(Turning back to **POPALOPALUS**.*)*

As I was saying…

(gasps in astonishment)

You are taller!

GIRAFFE. *(Looking down on* **LION**. *Starting to gain a little confidence.)* *Much* taller.

LION. You are thicker.

GIRAFFE. *Much* thicker.

LION. You are a great deal longer.

GIRAFFE. Very much longer! And my tail…

LION. *(looking off into the distance where the last* **ARMADILLO CHILD** *has disappeared)* There is no end to your tail!

(To **ZEBRA**.*)*

He did not look so big at first.

ZEBRA. He was sitting down.

OLD BABOON. It is time for me to judge. How many legs do you have?

LION. Four!

GIRAFFE. Eighty-six!

OLD BABOON. Heads?

LION. One!

GIRAFFE. Forty-three!

OLD BABOON. Teeth?

LION. Thirty-two!

GIRAFFE. Nine hundred and seventeen!

OLD BABOON. Tails?

LION. One!

GIRAFFE. One!

LION. Hah!

OLD BABOON. Length of tail?

LION. Three feet!

GIRAFFE. To quote Lion, there is no end to my tail.

OLD BABOON. The biggest animal is Popalopalus . . !

LION. *(cutting him off)* It doesn't matter who is bigger! It is strength that rules the jungle! Strength that chews the meat!

OLD BABOON. The second contest will be: who is strongest? The test is…

*(Handing them a vine, one end to **GIRAFFE** and one end to **LION**. The animals in the **POPALOPALUS** hold on to each other and get ready to pull.)*

Tug-of-war. There will be three tugs. Get ready, get set…pull!

*(**LION** pulls **POPALOPALUS** a few steps to the left. **LION**'s eyes are closed with the effort. **ZEBRA** directs more animals to join the **POPALOPALUS**. Some of the hiding animals jump up and join the "torso.")*

Pull!

*(**POPALOPALUS** pulls **LION** a few steps to the right, back to where they started. **LION**'s eyes are still closed. **ZEBRA** directs more animals to help. More of the hiding animals jump up and join the "torso.")*

Pull!

*(With one yank, **LION** is pulled all the way across the stage.)*

OLD BABOON. And the winner is…

LION. *(pretending to have let go of the vine)* No one! I let go! I became weary of the contest. Tug-of-war is foolish – a child's game. I refuse to play.

OLD BABOON. You have already played. And lost. Popalopalus is strongest.

*(**LION** glares. **OLD BABOON** ignores him.)*

And now the third and last contest: Who is loudest?

LION. No one large or small, strong or weak, new or old can out-roar Lion!

*(Takes throat spray from pocket, turns away as he sprays his throat. **ZEBRA** directs all the remaining animals to join the **POPALOPALUS**.)*

OLD BABOON. Are you ready, Lion?

LION. *(very confident)* Ready!

OLD BABOON. Are you ready, Popalopalus?

GIRAFFE. Ready!

LION. RRRRRROOOOAAAARRRR!!!

POPALOPALUS. RRRRRROOOOOOOOAAAAAAARRRRRRRRRRR!!!!!!!

LION. *(staggers back)* You have grown new mouths!

POPALOPALUS. RRRRRRRRRROOOOOOOOAAAAAAAAARRRRRRRRRRR!!!!!!!

LION. *(covering his ears)* Aaaah! It is too much!

POPALOPALUS. RRRRRRRRROOOOOOOOOOOAAAAAAARRRRRRRRRRRRRRRRR!!!!!!!!!

LION. *(cowering)* Stop! Oh stop! Please stop! You are the loudest thing I have ever heard!

OLD BABOON. And the winner is Popalopalus! He is biggest, strongest, loudest!

LION. *(in disbelief)* It is true. He has won and I, Lion, have lost. And so this corner of the jungle is his and not mine. I will go away now, leave this my home, find a new and empty corner of the jungle to be alone in…

(leaving sadly)

OLD BABOON. Lion – wait.

*(**LION** stops.)*

Perhaps the Popalopalus will not mind if you stay.

*(These characters speak as part of the **POPALOPALUS**.)*

SPIDER. I suppose this corner of the jungle must have a lion.

ANT. I would do it but it bores me.

BEETLE. So I do not mind if he stays as long as he does not roar between dusk and dawn.

TOUCAN. His roaring is not loud enough to keep me awake, of course, but it is small and whining like a mosquito.

PYTHON. It annoys me.

LION. *(ingratiating)* As you wish. I would never annoy such a fine new member of the jungle family. It is always my pleasure to accommodate a new animal, especially one with hundreds of mouths.

(A terrible thought. Even more ingratiating.)

There aren't any more of you, are there?

PARROT 1. I have thousands of cousins.

PARROT 2. I will write to them immediately if your pathetic roaring annoys me again.

PARROT 3. They will insist on visiting…

PARROT 4. *(a threat)* And they will all want to meet you.

LION. Oh no! One new animal at a time is all the pleasure I can stand.

MONKEY 1. And it is my pleasure to sleep through the jungle night undisturbed.

MONKEY 2. If my sleep is disturbed…

MONKEY 3. I can't tell you how hungry I get.

OLD BABOON. And, Popalopalus, what is it that you eat?

PARROT 5. Oh, nothing very interesting. I eat lions.

*(**LION** very afraid.)*

MONKEY 4. Oh, I don't eat lions all the time.

*(**LION** very relieved.)*

GIRAFFE. *(supremely confident, glaring down at **LION**)* Only when I'm *hungry*.

LION. *(very, very afraid)* How does one tell when a Popalopalus is hungry?

GIRAFFE. My tail starts to twitch.

*(**ARMADILLO** and **ARMADILLO CHILDREN** start moving back and forth in a nervous tail twitch.)*

LION. *(almost whispering now)* I must go home now and practice my whispering.

*(Runs away and off left. The very happy animals break up the **POPALOPALUS** and, as they talk, find their way back to their original places.)*

PARROT 5. Lion ran away!

SPIDER. And he took his teeth with him!

BEETLE. How did we think of so many wonderful lies?

ZEBRA. We were inspired!

OLD BABOON. Zebra, this inspiration of yours – it was not stupid.

(**ZEBRA** *looks proud.*)

This time.

(**ZEBRA** *looks a little humbled.* **OLD BABOON** *closes eyes. Animals are all getting comfortable, curling up, getting ready to go to sleep.*)

GIRAFFE. And the Lion will never know that the Popalopalus was…

PARROT 1. One…

(*Falls asleep. As the animals fall asleep, they all tilt their heads to the left.*)

PARROT 2. Two…

(*falls asleep*)

PARROT 3. Three…

(*falls asleep*)

PARROT 4. Four…

(*falls asleep*)

PARROT 5. Five parrots.

(*falls asleep*)

MONKEY 1. One…

(*falls asleep*)

MONKEY 2. Two…

(*falls asleep*)

MONKEY 3. Three…

(*falls asleep*)

MONKEY 4. Four monkeys.

(*falls asleep*)

HYENA 1. One…

(falls asleep)

HYENA 2. Two hyenas.

(falls asleep)

SPIDER. Spider.

(falls asleep)

ANT. Ant.

(falls asleep)

BEETLE. Beetle.

(falls asleep)

OSTRICH. Ostrich.

(falls asleep)

PYTHON. Python.

(falls asleep)

RHINOCEROS. Rhinoceros.

(falls asleep)

TOUCAN. Toucan.

(falls asleep)

GAZELLE. Gazelle.

(falls asleep)

GIRAFFE. Giraffe.

(falls asleep)

ANTELOPE. Antelope.

(falls asleep)

LEOPARD. Leopard.

(falls asleep)

ZEBRA. Zebra.

(falls asleep)

ARMADILLO. Armadillo.

(gathering her children in close to her)

ARMADILLO CHILD 1. And one…

(curling in close)

ARMADILLO CHILD 2. Two…

(curling in close)

ARMADILLO CHILD 3. Three…

(curling in close)

ARMADILLO CHILD 4. Four armadillo children.

(curling in close)

ARMADILLO. Who celebrated by sleeping through the long, silent jungle night. Good night…

(falls asleep)

ARMADILLO CHILD 1. Night…

*(falls asleep. As **ARMADILLO CHILDREN** go to sleep they rest their heads on the back of the **ARMADILLO CHILD** in front of them.)*

ARMADILLO CHILD 2. Night…

(falls asleep)

ARMADILLO CHILD 3. Night…

(falls asleep)

ARMADILLO CHILD 4. Night.

(falls asleep)

ALL. *(move their sleepy heads slowly from being tilted to the left to being tilted to the right)* Aaaaaaaaahhhhhhhh.

(All sound asleep and still.)

A FAIR PRICE

CHARACTERS

WOMAN	**CUSTOMER 1**
DAUGHTER	**CUSTOMER 2**
DRIVER	**CUSTOMER 3**
DONKEY	**CUSTOMER 4**
HEADWOMAN 1	**CUSTOMER 5**
BAKER	**CUSTOMER 6**
HEADWOMAN 2	**CUSTOMER 7**
PEDDLER	**CUSTOMER 8**
HEADWOMAN 3	

A NOTE ON CASTING

The play is written for a cast of 17. It may be performed by a cast of 9 with doubling. It may be performed by a cast larger than 17 by adding more CUSTOMERS.

None of the roles are gender specific. For example, HEADWOMAN may be played as HEADMAN.

COSTUMES

The cast wears black t-shirts, black pants and black socks to which they add:

FEMALE CHARACTERS wear long, colorful, brightly patterned skirts and scarves, none of which match. The scarves are tied snugly around their heads, all hair tucked up underneath.

MALE CHARACTERS wear brightly colored vests and hats none of which match.

DONKEY wears a dark-colored man's hat with donkey ears attached.

BAKER wears a white chef's hat and apron.

PROPS

Nine large copper coins
One scarf

(Cast, except **WOMAN** *and* **DAUGHTER**, *sits on the floor in a semicircle, facing audience.* **WOMAN** *stands left and* **DAUGHTER** *stands right in front of semicircle, facing audience.)*

WOMAN. *(sadly)* Ah, I'm lonely.

DAUGHTER. *(sadly)* Oh, I'm lonely.

WOMAN. *(indicating right)* I miss my daughter, away that way.

DAUGHTER. *(indicating left)* I miss my mother, away that way.

*(***WOMAN & DAUGHTER*** sigh lonely sighs.)*

WOMAN. *(glance down at her feet)* And here I got feet and there I got road…

(stepping on to road)

And so I'll walk it.

(walking from left to right, briskly for a few steps, then slower and with more effort)

Ah, it's a fierce road, sprung with holes and besotted with rocks and ditches deep and hills steep plus the legs is old and blistering fast and I'd fly if I could but can't…

(a last weary step)

Arrived!

DAUGHTER. Mother!

WOMAN. Daughter!

WOMAN & DAUGHTER. I missed you!

(They hug.)

DAUGHTER. Tea?

(Pours imaginary tea. They sip. Offering imaginary plate.)

Cookie?

*(***WOMAN*** takes one. Happily chatting.)*

Gossip…

WOMAN. Gossip…

DAUGHTER. Gossip…

WOMAN. Gossip…

WOMAN & DAUGHTER. *(having a wonderful time)* Gossip, gossip, gossip, gossip, gossip!

(Happy sigh. Both take a final sip of tea, use hems of skirts as napkins to delicately dab mouths and fingertips.)

WOMAN. *(sadly)* Time to go.

WOMAN & DAUGHTER. I'll miss you!

*(Hug. **WOMAN** faces left. **DAUGHTER** sits in semicircle, wiping away a tear.)*

WOMAN. *(peering down at road)* And here's the road means to eat me alive.

(a worried and weary sigh)

DRIVER. *(coming forward, **DONKEY** beside him)* Trouble, missus?

WOMAN. It's this road chewed me up this morning and my two legs not the least recovered from the ordeal and got to go another round with it.

DRIVER. No need, missus. I got a cart here. I got a donkey pulls the cart. And all of us – cart, donkey and myself – hire out.

WOMAN. Do you?

DRIVER. We do.

WOMAN. Do you hire out to go down this road away that way?

(pointing left)

DRIVER. We do. And a cart ride's easy on your legs.

WOMAN. Is it?

DRIVER. It is. For its the donkey's four legs do the work, while these other four legs belonging to us do nothing.

WOMAN. Do you charge?

DRIVER. I do.

WOMAN. How much do you charge?

DRIVER. Three copper coins.

WOMAN. A fair price.

DRIVER. It is.
WOMAN. Agreed.
DRIVER. Agreed.
> *(helps **WOMAN** step up into an imaginary cart)*

So up you go.

> *(Gets up on cart himself. **DONKEY** is in position to pull cart.)*

And up I go. And off we go…

> *(taking up imaginary reins)*

Gidyup.

> *(**WOMAN**, **DRIVER**, **DONKEY** moving to center.)*

ALL. Ride, ride, ride.
DRIVER. *(looking up and squinting)* Sun high.
WOMAN. *(nodding in agreement)* High.
DRIVER. Sun hot.
WOMAN. *(nodding in agreement)* Hot.
WOMAN, DRIVER, DONKEY. *(wilting in the heat)* Whoooo!
DRIVER. *(pulling back on reins)* Whoa!

> *(Stop.)*

I got to water and rest my beast. For a donkey'll tip in the heat. It's happened before.

> *(Getting down from cart. Offers imaginary containers to **DONKEY**.)*

Gabble of grain…

> *(A noisy gulp or two as **DONKEY** eats.)*

Garble of water…

> *(A noisy slurp as **DONKEY** drinks.)*

And now we got to let him rest and digest. For an undigested donkey'll explode. It's happened before. And I myself don't mind some shade.

> *(As he sits on floor and slides back under the cart.)*

And there ain't tree nor shrub for miles, so it's under the cart where the only shade to be had is to be had.

WOMAN. *(steps down from cart)* I myself don't mind some shade.

(sits on floor and slides back under the cart)

DRIVER, WOMAN, DONKEY, ALL. Aaaahhhhh.

WOMAN. Shade.

DRIVER. Cool.

WOMAN. Rest.

DONKEY. Digest.

WOMAN, DRIVER, DONKEY, ALL. *(contented sighs)*

DRIVER. *(getting up)* And up.

WOMAN. *(getting up)* Up.

DRIVER. *(steps up on to cart.)* And on.

WOMAN. *(steps up on to cart)* On.

DRIVER. And off.

(gives reins a snap)

Gidyup.

*(**WOMAN**, **DRIVER**, **DONKEY** moving to left.)*

ALL. Ride, ride, ride.

DRIVER. *(at left where **WOMAN** started)* Arrived!

*(Stop. **WOMAN** and **DRIVER** step down from cart.)*

WOMAN. Ah, good to be home. I thank you for the convenience of the ride. And now I owe you the price of the ride.

DRIVER. You do.

WOMAN. And here it is.

(taking three coins from pocket)

Three copper coins.

*(counts out the coins, laying each one on **DRIVER**'s outstretched hand)*

One, two, three.

DRIVER. *(hand remains out)* And three more besides.

WOMAN. Three and only three was the agreed upon price.

DRIVER. Three and only three was the agreed upon price of your ride in the cart.

WOMAN. And there they all are counted out for you.

(pointing to each coin)

One, two, three!

DRIVER. And the three more besides is the price for your use of the shade beneath the cart.

WOMAN. Are you mad?

DRIVER. I'm not!

WOMAN. You are! Nobody charges nobody for sitting in the shade!

DRIVER. I do when the shade is under my cart, the cart being my personal property as is the shade manufactured by it.

WOMAN. We'll see what Headwoman of the town has to say about that! We'll just see! And me off to find her!

(Walking in a fast, angry circle. **DRIVER** *is right at her heels.* **DONKEY** *is right at* **DRIVER***'s heels.)*

DRIVER. And me on your heels!

DONKEY. And me on his heels!

HEADWOMAN 1. *(Has stood and come forward. Stops* **WOMAN**, **DRIVER** *and* **DONKEY** *at center.)* I've a brain pointy and sharp so am Headwoman of the town.

WOMAN. Madam, I do you honor.

(a respectful bow)

HEADWOMAN 1. I appreciate the honor.

(a respectful nod.)

WOMAN. And I ask the favor of a judgment against this thief here.

DRIVER. I ain't no thief. I'm a cart driver got to be paid what's fair.

HEADWOMAN 1. Tell me the trouble.

WOMAN. Here to away that way. Walk. Away that way to here. Cart.

ALL. Ride, ride, ride.

WOMAN. Three copper coins agreed upon. Shade. Rest. Arrived. Three copper coins paid. And three more besides!

HEADWOMAN 1. For what?

WOMAN. For sitting in the shade of the cart!

DRIVER. The three copper coins agreed upon is for the ride only. The three more besides is a charge for use of the shade of the cart which was in no way included in the original bargain. I got to be paid what's fair!

HEADWOMAN 1. And you will be. For I know what's fair.

WOMAN. Do you?

HEADWOMAN 1. I do.

WOMAN. And how do you know?

HEADWOMAN 1. Here's how.

>   *(**WOMAN**, **DRIVER** and **DONKEY** sit in semicircle.)*
>
>   It was a day like any day and me at market and all a-twitch at the astonishments of it. There was singers of songs…

ALL. La!

HEADWOMAN 1. Dancers and drummers…

ALL. Ah!

HEADWOMAN 1. Tellers of tales and misfortunes and lies…

ALL. Oh!

HEADWOMAN 1. Enchanters! Bedazzlers! Evangelizers!

ALL. Oooh!

HEADWOMAN 1. *(the best of all)* And food!

ALL. Um!

HEADWOMAN 1. *(rhapsodizing)* Ah, the food! Oh, the food! Cream puffs! Dumplings! Sausages! Sugar cakes, cream cakes, custard cakes. Ah, but it's…

BAKER. *(Coming forward. Announcing his wares.)* Honey cakes! Sticky and sweet!

HEADWOMAN 1. I set my heart on.

ALL. *(get up and form a line from right to left, all facing **BAKER**. To **HEADWOMAN 1**.)* Loooooong line.

HEADWOMAN 1. *(walking down line to the end of it)* I don't mind it's long cause of the honey cake waiting at the end.

ALL. *(To **HEADWOMAN 1**.)* Slooooow line.

HEADWOMAN 1. *(taking her place at the end of the line)* I don't mind it's slow cause of the honey cake waiting at the end.

ALL. Long. Slow. Long. Slow. Long. Slow. Long.

(With each word, the line moves ahead one slow step. As each person gets to the front of line, he pays **BAKER** *imaginary coin, receives an imaginary honey cake, hurries back to semicircle to sit and eat it.)*

HEADWOMAN 1. *(steps to front of line)* One honey cake please.

BAKER. Just sold out the last one.

HEADWOMAN 1. *(great disappointment)* Ah. I'm slumped.

(Slumps. Turning to leave.)

BAKER. *(holding out hand)* That'll be three copper coins.

HEADWOMAN 1. *(turning back)* But you said you sold out.

BAKER. I have. But haven't you been there in that line a long time?

HEADWOMAN 1. I was. And a long slow time it was. I thought I'd tip from the strain. But I knew how a honey cake'd be worth the struggle so I kept at it.

BAKER. And what were you doing that whole long slow time in line?

HEADWOMAN 1. Why, just standing there in a decent orderly fashion, as I was brung up by my parents to do.

BAKER. And while you was being so orderly and decent, did you smell my honey cakes at all?

HEADWOMAN 1. I did. It was what kept me going. It's the smell what lent me hope.

BAKER. And the charge for the smell of my honey cakes is three copper coins.

HEADWOMAN 1. Are you mad?

BAKER. I'm not!

HEADWOMAN 1. You are! Nobody charges nobody for the smell of a honey cake!

BAKER. I do. The honey cakes is my own personal property and their smells, being a result of the honey cakes, is the same and can be charged for.

HEADWOMAN 1. We'll see what Headwoman of the town says about that! We'll just see! And me tracking her down!

(Walking in a fast, angry circle. **BAKER** *is right at her heels.)*

BAKER. And me on your heels!

(HEADWOMAN 2 *stands and comes forward. Stops* **HEADWOMAN 1** *and* **BAKER** *at center.)*

HEADWOMAN 2. I've a brain full of wires that work so am Headwoman of the town.

HEADWOMAN 1. Madam, honor to your office!

(quick respectful bow)

HEADWOMAN 2. Honor appreciated.

(quick respectful nod)

HEADWOMAN 1. And I ask a judgment against this thief here.

BAKER. I ain't a thief. I'm a baker got to be paid what's fair.

HEADWOMAN 2. Tell the trouble.

HEADWOMAN 1. Market. Astonishments.

ALL. La-ah-oh-oooh-um!

HEADWOMAN 1. Honey cakes. Line. Long. Slow. Sold out. Three copper coins!

HEADWOMAN 2. For what?

HEADWOMAN 1. For the smell of the cakes I smelt whilst in the line!

BAKER. Some of the deliciousness of the honey cakes is contained in the smell of them. And it's for that I got to be paid what's fair!

HEADWOMAN 2. And you will be. For I know what's fair.

HEADWOMAN 1. Do you?

HEADWOMAN 2. I do.

HEADWOMAN 1. And how do you know?

HEADWOMAN 2. Here's how.

(HEADWOMAN 1 *and* **BAKER** *sit in semicircle.)*

ALL. *(This isn't good news.)* Again?

HEADWOMAN 2. Again.

ALL. Are you sure?

HEADWOMAN 2. I am.

ALL. *(resigned)* Here's how.

HEADWOMAN 2. It was a day like any day and me set on stoop to drink my breakfast tea as I done every morning of my blessed and blameless life.

PEDDLER. *(comes forward)* Peddler!

HEADWOMAN 2. Waddaya peddling?

PEDDLER. *(setting out imaginary wares)* My pots. My pans. My cups. My cummerbunds. My cuzzles and buzzles and frimfraws and gimricks. And now the crowd.

(yelling to draw a crowd)

Pots and pans and cups and cummerbunds and cuzzles and buzzles and frimfraws and gimricks!

(CUSTOMERS *jumping up and crowding around with great excitement.)*

CUSTOMER 1. *(spying a treasure)* I'll take that pot there!

(pays, picks up pot, hurries back to semicircle, sits)

CUSTOMER 2. *(pointing)* Gimme that pan!

(PEDDLER *does. Pays, takes it, runs back to semicircle, sits.)*

CUSTOMER 3. *(grabbing it)* I got to have a cuzzle!

(pays, takes it, runs back to semicircle, sits)

CUSTOMER 4. *(very demanding)* Two buzzles! Big ones! None of them little puny ones!

(PEDDLER *hands over something huge. Pays, struggles a bit as he carries it back to semicircle, sits.)*

CUSTOMER 5. *(timid)* A gimrick and a half!

(PEDDLER *hands over something little. Pays, slips it in pocket, goes back to semicircle, sits.)*

CUSTOMER 6. *(refusing to be ignored any longer)* I'll have the red frimfraw!

(**PEDDLER** *hands it over. Pays, goes back to semicircle, admiring his purchase, sits.*)

CUSTOMER 7. *(not to be outdone)* And I'll have the big purple one next to it.

(**PEDDLER** *hands it over. Pays, heads back to semicircle, makes sure everyone notices his purchase, sits.*)

CUSTOMER 8. *(All the other **CUSTOMERS** are seated. Pointing.)* What's that there way down under all the rest?

PEDDLER. *(Sees what he's pointing at. Pulls out an imaginary flute. Holds it up.)* A flute.

CUSTOMER 8. What's a flute do?

PEDDLER. Why, it plays mellifluous music.

(plays the flute by whistling a little tune)

CUSTOMER 8. *(enchanted)* Why, it is mellifluous. My little girl back at home better have that.

PEDDLER. *(holding out hand)* Price.

CUSTOMER 8. *(puts imaginary coin in **PEDDLER**'s hand)* Paid.

PEDDLER. *(holding out flute)* Flute.

CUSTOMER 8. *(Taking flute. Toots a little toot by whistling. Delighted.)* And I'll dance it home.

(Returns to semicircle, playing the flute – whistling a little tune – and dancing a step or two on the way, sits.)

HEADWOMAN 2. *(drains cup)* Ah, cup empty. Tea drunk.

(turning to leave)

Floor needs a sweep, dish needs a swish…

PEDDLER. *(going to **HEADWOMAN 2**)* Hold on there!

(hand outstretched)

That'll be three copper coins.

HEADWOMAN 2. Who you talking to? It ain't me?

PEDDLER. It's you. Pay up, sister.

HEADWOMAN 2. I ain't your sister and I bought nothing.

PEDDLER. But you sat there the whole time with your ears wide open letting the melluflious music of the flute slide down into them.

HEADWOMAN 2. I sat and drank my tea and whatever noise there was there was.

PEDDLER. And the charge for the noise of the flute is three copper coins.

HEADWOMAN 2. Are you mad?

PEDDLER. I'm not!

HEADWOMAN 2. You are! For nobody charges nobody for a noise!

PEDDLER. I do. The noise of the flute being what makes the thing operational, I got to charge for it. I got to be paid what's fair.

HEADWOMAN 2. We'll see what Headwoman of the town says about that!

ALL. We'll just see!

HEADWOMAN 2. And me off to dig her up!

(Walking in fast, angry circle. **PEDDLER** *is right at her heels.)*

ALL. And him on her heels!

HEADWOMAN 3. *(Coming forward. Stops* **HEADWOMAN 2** *and* **PEDDLER** *at center.)* I've a brain full of glorious light so am Headwoman of the town.

HEADWOMAN 2. Honors!

(very quick respectful bow)

HEADWOMAN 3. Appreciated!

(very quick respectful nod)

HEADWOMAN 2. Thief!

PEDDLER. Ain't!

HEADWOMAN 3. Tell!

HEADWOMAN 2. Stoop. Tea. Peddler sets up.

ALL. Potspanscupscumberbundscuzzlesbuzzlesfrimfrawsgimricksflute!

HEADWOMAN 2. Plays as requested by customer. Purchase. Leaves. Three copper coins!

HEADWOMAN 3. For what?

HEADWOMAN 2. For hearing the noise of the flute!

PEDDLER. The flute being my personal property at the time, what noises float out of it is the same. I got to be paid what's fair!

ALL. And you know what she says. She says…

HEADWOMAN 3. And you will be. For I know what's fair.

HEADWOMAN 2. Do you?

HEADWOMAN 3. I do.

HEADWOMAN 2. And how do you know?

HEADWOMAN 3. Here's how.

ALL. *(Heads sink down into hands. A discouraged groan.)* Aaaaaaaahhhh.

HEADWOMAN 3. Tragically, I got no time to tell you now…

ALL. *(Heads pop up. Happy relief.)* Aaaaaaaaaaaah!

HEADWOMAN 3. But I got time to show you.

> *(to* **HEADWOMAN 2***)*
>
> You didn't buy the flute?

HEADWOMAN 2. I didn't.

HEADWOMAN 3. And the noise of the flute just floated over and sunk into your ears?

HEADWOMAN 2. It did.

HEADWOMAN 3. And you didn't no ways encourage it?

HEADWOMAN 2. I didn't.

HEADWOMAN 3. *(to* **PEDDLER***)* You didn't sell her the flute?

PEDDLER. I didn't. Some other lady long gone committed the purchase of the flute.

HEADWOMAN 3. And you charged this other long gone lady what for the purchase of the flute?

PEDDLER. Three copper coins.

HEADWOMAN 3. So it's three copper coins for the actuality of the flute?

PEDDLER. It is.

HEADWOMAN 3. And now I'll judge.

> *(Thinks hard. To* **PEDDLER***.)*
>
> I judge you got to be paid what's fair.

PEDDLER. *(triumphantly)* Ha!

HEADWOMAN 2. *(very disappointed)* Ah.

HEADWOMAN 3. And here's what's fair.

(to **HEADWOMAN 2**)

Have you three copper coins?

HEADWOMAN 2. I have.

(taking coins from pocket)

HEADWOMAN 3. Have you a scarf?

HEADWOMAN 2. I have.

(taking scarf from pocket)

HEADWOMAN 3. Tie them up, the coins in the scarf.

HEADWOMAN 2. *(tying coins loosely in scarf)* Done.

HEADWOMAN 3. Give them a shake.

HEADWOMAN 2. *(Gives coins a shake. They make a loud, rattling noise.)* There it is.

HEADWOMAN 3. As the cost of the flute is three copper coins, the cost of the noise of the flute is the noise of three copper coins. Go ahead.

(**HEADWOMAN 2** *continues rattling coins. To* **PEDDLER**.)

As to how long the noise should go on, I leave it to you. Say so when you're paid up.

PEDDLER. *(pushes away scarf and coins in disgust)* Bah!

HEADWOMAN 2. *(happy)* Ah!

(**PEDDLER** *walks angrily back to semicircle, scowling.* **HEADWOMAN 2** *bows respectfully to* **HEADWOMAN 3**. **HEADWOMAN 3** *nods politely in response and returns to semicircle.*)

HEADWOMAN 2. *(as* **HEADWOMAN 1** *and* **BAKER** *join her)* And that's how I know what's fair.

(to **HEADWOMAN 1**)

So you didn't buy a honey cake?

HEADWOMAN 1. I didn't.

HEADWOMAN 2. *(to* **BAKER**) You didn't sell her a honey cake?

BAKER. I didn't.

HEADWOMAN 2. And the cost of a honey cake on the occasion such a honey cake is available?

BAKER. Three copper coins.

HEADWOMAN 2. And now I'll judge.

(Thinks hard. To BAKER.)

I judge you got to be paid what's fair.

BAKER. *(triumphantly)* Hah!

HEADWOMAN 1. *(very disappointed)* Ah.

HEADWOMAN 2. And here's what's fair.

(to HEADWOMAN 1)

Do you have three copper coins?

HEADWOMAN 1. I do.

(takes coins out of pocket)

HEADWOMAN 2. Hold them out in your open hand there.

(HEADWOMAN 1 *does. Positioning* **HEADWOMAN 1***'s hand level with and close to* **BAKER***'s nose.)*

A bit up, a bit up…and level off there. As the cost of the honey cake was three copper coins, the cost of the smell of the honey cake is the smell of three copper coins. And there they are – available for smelling.

(to BAKER)

As to the length of the smell, I leave it to you. Tell us when you're paid up.

BAKER. *(pushing away* **HEADWOMAN 1***'s hand in disgust)* Bah!

HEADWOMAN 1. *(happy)* Ah!

(BAKER *walks angrily back to semicircle, scowling.* **HEADWOMAN 1** *bows respectfully to* **HEADWOMAN 2**. **HEADWOMAN 2** *nods politely in response and returns to semicircle.)*

HEADWOMAN 1. *(as* **WOMAN**, **DRIVER** *and* **DONKEY** *join her)* And that's how I know what's fair.

(to WOMAN)

You agreed to a price for your ride in the cart?

WOMAN. I did.

HEADWOMAN 1. *(to* **DRIVER***)* And you agreed when she agreed?

DRIVER. I did.

*(***DONKEY** *nodding in agreement.)*

HEADWOMAN 1. And the price agreed upon was?

WOMAN & DRIVER. Three copper coins.

HEADWOMAN 1. *(to* **WOMAN***)* How much of the three did you pay?

WOMAN. All three!

HEADWOMAN 1. *(to* **DRIVER***)* You got them handy?

DRIVER. I do.

HEADWOMAN 1. I got to see them.

DRIVER. *(holding out coins)* There they are.

HEADWOMAN 1. And now I'll judge.

(Thinks hard. To **DRIVER***.)*

I judge you got to be paid what's fair.

DRIVER. *(triumphantly)* Hah!

WOMAN. *(very disappointed)* Ah.

HEADWOMAN 1. And here's what's fair.

(to **DRIVER***)*

Do you see the sun?

(pointing up)

*(***DRIVER** *and* **DONKEY** *looking up, squinting.)*

DRIVER. I do.

HEADWOMAN 1. Do you see the ground?

(pointing down)

*(***DRIVER** *and* **DONKEY** *looking down.)*

DRIVER. I do.

HEADWOMAN 1. Hold the coins between the two.

DRIVER. *(holds coins between his fingers, stretching his arm out so coins are between sun and ground)* There they are.

HEADWOMAN 1. As the cost of riding in the cart is three copper coins, the cost of the shadow of the cart is the shadow of three copper coins.

(pointing at the ground. To **DRIVER.***)*

And there they are. Help yourself.

DRIVER. *(pulling back hand in disgust)* Bah!

WOMAN. *(happy)* Ah!

*(***DRIVER** *and* **DONKEY** *walk angrily back to semicircle, scowling.* **WOMAN** *bows respectfully to* **HEADWOMAN 1**. **HEADWOMAN 1** *nods politely in response and returns to semicircle.)*

WOMAN. And that's…

(All come forward, form a line facing the audience.)

ALL. A fair price.

(bow heads)

BANANA SANDWICH IN A BOAT

CHARACTERS

MAN
FATHER
DAUGHTER
MAN 2
WIFE
MOTHER
WOMAN
HOUSE 1, 2, 3, 4, 5, 6, 7, 8

WEDDING GUEST 1
WEDDING GUEST 2
BRIDE
WEDDING GUEST 3
WEDDING GUEST 4
TOWN CRIER
PRIEST

A NOTE ON CASTING

The play is written for a cast of 22. It may be performed by a cast of 12 with doubling. It may be performed by a cast larger than 22 by adding to HOUSE or WEDDING GUESTS.

The script requires 2 men (MAN and MAN 1) and 2 women (DAUGHTER and BRIDE). The other roles are not gender specific. For example, FATHER may be played as MOTHER.

COSTUMES

All cast members wear black t-shirts, black pants and black socks. Add costume pieces with lots of bright colors, fringes, ruffles, tassels and other whimsically decorative touches:

MAN, FATHER: Tunics and matching hats.

DAUGHTER, BRIDE: Frilly aprons, bridal veils.

MAN 1: Baggy pants and matching hat.

WIFE, MOTHER: Aprons and matching kerchiefs tied over hair.

WOMAN: Apron with large pocket and matching hat.

HOUSE: Brown hoods.

WEDDING GUESTS, TOWN CRIER: Tunics and matching hats for men. Aprons and matching hats for women.

PRIEST: Black robe and black hat with a clerical look.

PROPS

Two bridal bouquets
A pair of oversized pants
An old bucket
Stick to use as a slicer
A door knob
Broom handle decorated with flowers and ribbons
A hand bell
Three dolls, the size of newborns, wrapped in blankets

SET

A sturdy chair with a back. May be painted bright colors.

(Chair right. **MAN, FATHER** *and* **DAUGHTER** *standing in line at center with their backs to the audience.* **FATHER** *is center,* **MAN** *is left,* **DAUGHTER** *is right.)*

MAN. *(Turns to face audience. To* **FATHER***. Respectful but determined.)* Sir!

FATHER. *(Turns to face audience. To* **MAN***. Polite but not especially interested.)* Sir.

MAN. *(a standard greeting)* Does the day find you, sir?

FATHER. *(a standard response)* It does.

MAN. Here's a request.

FATHER. I'll hear it.

MAN. I ask the job of marrying your daughter.

FATHER. I've a trove of daughters. Which?

MAN. *(Pointing to* **DAUGHTER***. In love.)* That. With her starry eyes and enchanting heart and I loved her since a lad.

FATHER. Daughter.

DAUGHTER. *(Turns to face audience. To* **FATHER***.)* Father?

FATHER. This fella says marriage.

DAUGHTER. To?

FATHER. You. Will you be married?

DAUGHTER. *(in love)* I will. For he's prince of my heart and I loved him since a lass.

FATHER. And so betrothed. And wedding'll be?

MAN. *(very sure)* Today at the latest.

FATHER. So soon?

DAUGHTER. *(very sure)* Love don't trot, Father, but gallops straight ahead.

FATHER. And off a cliff, often enough. But so be it. Daughter, array yourself.

*(***DAUGHTER***, very happy, exits right.)*

MAN. Ah, to be married. Gives my heart the jumps. What a cozy life we'll have. Me and the wife in the cottage with the garden and the gate and a fidget of smoke from out the chimney. And in a year's time, with heaven on our side, there'll be the firstborn child.

FATHER. There will.

MAN. And, boy or girl, name of child will be…

(with great pride and joy)

Banana Sandwich In A Boat!

FATHER. *(couldn't have heard that right)* This ear is prone to blockage.

(leaning in and cupping one ear)

Say again.

MAN. *(happy to repeat it)* Banana Sandwich In A Boat!

FATHER. *(still not right)* Try this other one.

(leaning in and cupping other ear)

MAN. *(slower and louder)* Banana Sandwich In A Boat!

FATHER. *(still not right)* Both together.

(leaning in and cupping both ears)

MAN. *(very loudly and very clearly enunciated)* Child's name will be Banana Sandwich In A Boat!

DAUGHTER. *(entering wearing veil and carrying bouquet)* And here I am arrayed…

FATHER. *(adamant)* Wedding's off!

DAUGHTER. *(horrified)* Ah! What can you mean?!

FATHER. As I'm father and boss of the world and on investigation man proves a fool, wedding's off.

DAUGHTER. But I love him past peace!

FATHER. He aims to name firstborn child…

(can hardly bear to say it)

Banana Sandwich In A Boat, proving he's the greatest fool of the world and I won't have him in the family.

MAN. I'm astonished at your innocence, sir. Have you never been out in the world?

FATHER. I have.

MAN. And whilst out in it, have you never met a fool?

FATHER. Not so great as yourself.

MAN. Why, the earth is flabbergasted in fools greater than me. Greater fools than me is common as paste. The ground runs thick with them. I myself trip over a dozen a day without trying.

FATHER. Do you?

MAN. I do.

FATHER. *(makes him a deal)* Then here it is: You go out into the world and find three fools greater than yourself and wedding's on. If not, not.

MAN. Word?

FATHER. Word.

> *(MAN and FATHER shake hands.)*

And so law.

MAN. *(not the least bit worried)* Easy as butter.

> *(To DAUGHTER.)*

We'll be married by setting sun. Be assured of it. And me off into the world.

FATHER. *(lining up next to MAN)* And me behind to witness.

DAUGHTER. *(Not quite trusting FATHER. Lining up next to FATHER.)* And me behind to witness the witnessing.

MAN, FATHER, DAUGHTER. And up and off and round the town we walk, we walk, we walk...

> *(Walk in circle and end up right where MAN 1, WIFE and MOTHER have entered. WIFE and MOTHER carry on oversized pants. MAN 1 stands on chair. WIFE and MOTHER kneel in front of chair, holding out pants between them.)*

MAN 1. *(has taken aim and is about to jump off the chair)* And...

MAN. *(stopping MAN from jumping)* Pardon, sir, any fools about?

MAN 1. *(Removing hat. Very respectful.)* Oh no, sir, not a one. For fools is unlawful and we won't put up with them.

(Puts hat back on.)

And…

(Aims. Jumps. Misses pants.)

Beans and noodles! Missed by a mile!

(Returns to chair, limping a little, rubbing back.)

MOTHER. *(Giving* **MAN 1** *an encouraging pat as he passes.)* A brave effort, son.

WIFE. *(Organizing the pants, giving them a good hard shake.)* Don't mind it, husband. The things is twitchy.

MOTHER. *(Gives* **MAN 1** *a little boost as he gets back on chair.)* Up again into your tree.

MAN 1. And…

(An elaborate new way of aiming. Jumps. Misses.)

Noodles and beans! Missed again!

(returning to chair, a little slower this time)

MOTHER. It sank right, son.

WIFE. And lifted left.

(Licks finger. Checks wind.)

Mind the wind now.

*(***MOTHER** *and* **WIFE** *shake out pants as a team, exchanging places, busily repositioning pants.)*

MOTHER. Trousers go ballooning in a wind.

WIFE. A ballooning trouser is a dicey thing.

MOTHER. A ballooning trouser can turn on you and knock you into next Tuesday.

*(***WIFE** *and* **MOTHER** *finally settled, pants ready.)*

MAN 1. *(Has taken elaborate new aim. Ready to jump.)* And…

MAN. *(stopping* **MAN 1** *from jumping)* Pardon again, sir.

MAN 1. *(Hat off. Very respectful.)* At your service.

MAN. And what's the purpose of your exercise?

MAN 1. Simple as bread. Have you never seen a man putting on his trousers?

MAN. I have.

MAN 1. Well, sir, you're seeing it again. I got new trousers need putting on and today's the day I pounce into them. I got this tree here for the launching plus I got the wife and the mother holding the hinges so...

(putting on hat)

It's up and aim and...

(Jumps. Misses.)

WIFE & MOTHER. *(sink back in disappointment)* Ah.

FATHER. So you mean to land in your trousers then?

MAN 1. *(limping, rubbing back)* I do, sir. I'm counting on it.

DAUGHTER. How long you been at it?

MAN 1. Oh, a terrible long time.

(a slow, sore climb back on to chair)

WIFE. *(a sad litany)* Kettle's boiled dry.

MOTHER. Fire's out.

WIFE. Dog's hungry.

MOTHER. Cat's starved.

WIFE. All resulting from the recalcitrance of the trousers.

MOTHER. Trousers ain't a reliable target.

WIFE. *(very sure of it)* We blame the trousers.

MAN 1. *(Elaborate aim. Ready to jump.)* And...

MAN. *(stopping **MAN 1** from jumping)* Sir, have you never put trousers on before?

MAN 1. Certainly I have. Ain't I wearing trousers?

MAN. And how'd you get in them?

MAN 1. Same way as this. But now these trousers is thin and worn to aggravation so I'm obliged to leap into a new pair. And...

(Jumps. Misses.)

WIFE & MOTHER. *(More disappointment. Slump back.)* Ah.

MAN. How do you get the old ones off?

MAN 1. *(can't believe his ears)* Off?! Are you mad? It's hard as blazes jumping into the things! It's near impossible to jump out of them! I about broke my neck trying!

MOTHER. *(another sad litany)* Plus busted a leg.

WIFE. Smashed a rib.

MOTHER. Wrinkled a ankle.

WIFE. Sprang a wrist.

MAN 1. *(noble)* A man got to suffer wants his trousers.

(getting back on chair)

WIFE. So once on, always on.

MOTHER. Just layer them up.

MAN 1. *(Standing on chair. A proud and noble figure.)* I'm wearing all the previous trousers of my life.

WIFE. *(prouder)* And it ain't every man can say that.

MAN. *(can stand no more of this foolishness)* And here's the end of it!

(taking trousers)

Give them over. Now look.

(putting one leg in trousers)

One leg in. So.

MAN 1, WIFE, MOTHER. *(Watching closely. Very confused.)* So?

MAN. *(putting other leg in trousers)* Other leg in. So.

MAN 1, WIFE, MOTHER. *(even more confused)* So?

MAN. On.

MAN 1, WIFE, MOTHER. *(staggered with amazement)* On!

WIFE. *(A little scared and nervous. To MOTHER.)* Magic.

MOTHER. *(Just as scared and nervous. To WIFE.)* Or something wicked similar.

MAN. Plus reverse takes them off.

MAN 1, WIFE, MOTHER. *(absolute and utter disbelief)* Never!

MAN. *(takes one leg out of trousers)* One leg off. So.

MAN 1, WIFE, MOTHER. *(more disbelief)* So?

MAN. *(taking other leg out)* Other leg off. So.

MAN 1, WIFE, MOTHER. *(even more disbelief)* So?

MAN. Off.

MAN 1, WIFE, MOTHER. *(astonished)* Off!

MAN 1. *(Stepping down from chair. Very brave.)* I'll take a try.

MAN. *(handing over trousers)* There they are. Teach them a lesson.

MAN 1. *(slowly and carefully puts one leg in trousers)* One leg in.

WIFE & MOTHER. *(Hopeful and nervous. Wringing hands.)* In…

MAN 1. *(slowly and carefully puts other leg in trousers)* Other leg in.

WIFE, MOTHER. *(More hopeful and nervous. Clinging to each other.)* In…

MAN 1. *(thrilled)* On!

WIFE, MOTHER. *(even more thrilled)* On!

(**WIFE** and **MOTHER** *doing a dance step or two as they go off.*)

WIFE. Time to start the fire!

MOTHER. Feed the dog!

WIFE. Acquire a kettle!

MOTHER. Resuscitate the cat!

MAN 1. *(dancing off behind them)* And I ain't jumping out of no more trees what ain't on fire!

(**MAN 1**, **WIFE** and **MOTHER** *exit right.*)

MAN. And there go three fools greater than me, making me a married man!

*(happily taking **DAUGHTER**'s hand)*

FATHER. *(Removing **DAUGHTER**'s hand from **MAN**, stepping between them.)* Nothing like it. I'm counting main fools only. That wife and that mother, being auxiliary fools, won't be calculated.

MAN. *(won't be deterred)* So that's one fool counted.

DAUGHTER. *(more determined than ever)* And two fools to be found.

MAN, FATHER, DAUGHTER. And up and off and round the town we walk, we walk, we walk…

(Walk in a circle, picking up chair and placing it left, as **WOMAN** *and* **HOUSE** *enter left.* **WOMAN** *is carrying bucket and has slicer – a long stick – in apron pocket.* **WOMAN** *sits on chair, sets bucket on floor, starts to cry loudly.* **HOUSE** *forms a rectangle to left of* **WOMAN**, *each with one arm raised to rest their hand on their neighbor's shoulder. The* **HOUSE** *cast member at the front holds a door knob at waist level and is, therefore, the door.)*

MAN. *(notices* **WOMAN***)* Pardon, missus, any fools about?

WOMAN. *(pauses in her crying)* Not a one, sir, for we don't let fools run loose.

(continues crying)

MAN. And what's the heartbreak?

WOMAN. Do you see my house there?

MAN, FATHER, DAUGHTER. We do.

WOMAN. Do you see the four scrumptious walls with not a hole in them?

MAN, FATHER, DAUGHTER. We do.

WOMAN. And the roof above? And the floor below? And the fine toothsome door sliced in?

FATHER. We all see all of it.

WOMAN. Ah, it's the finest house alive and useless all at once.

FATHER. Is it?

WOMAN. *(standing and taking* **FATHER** *to* **HOUSE***)* It is. Take a trip in.

(opens **HOUSE***'s door)*

HOUSE. Creeeeeaaaak!

WOMAN. *(gives* **FATHER** *a gentle shove in)* Shut up door.

(closing door behind him)

HOUSE. Creeeeeaaaak!

WOMAN. *(yelling)* What do you see?

FATHER. *(yelling)* Why, not a thing and plenty of it!

(opening door)

HOUSE. Creeeeeaaaaak!

*(**FATHER** steps out. Shuts door.)*

Creeeaaaak!

WOMAN. *(sinks on to chair)* And after me tossing in bucket after bucket of sunshine.

(crying)

FATHER. *(in disbelief)* You haven't.

WOMAN. *(jumps to her feet)* I'll prove it!

(holding up bucket for inspection)

Bucket.

(making a big, sweeping motion with it)

A big, fine swoosh of sunshine in it.

*(as she goes to **HOUSE**)*

Sunshine ain't no trouble to haul. Goes in bucket voluntarily. Don't weigh a feather.

(opens door)

HOUSE. Creeeeeaaaaak!

WOMAN. *(emptying bucket with a grand gesture)* And in!

(slams door)

HOUSE. Creeeeeaaaaak!

WOMAN. Wait whilst it flims and flams about. And…

*(grabs **FATHER**, opens door)*

HOUSE. Creeeeeaaaaak!

WOMAN. *(giving **FATHER** a gentle shove in)* In you go!

(shuts door)

HOUSE. Creeeeeaaaaak!

WOMAN. *(yelling)* And what's the report?

FATHER. *(yelling)* Black as night with both eyes closed!

(opens door)

HOUSE. Creeeeeaaaaak!

*(**FATHER** steps out. Shuts door.)*

Creeeeaaaaak!

WOMAN. *(distraught)* Same every time.

(collapses on to chair, crying)

FATHER. *(in disbelief)* And that's your heartbreak?

WOMAN. *(a pause in the crying)* It is. Plus I set my heart on skinning a cabbage for supper if I had a cabbage which I don't cause I'm too busy bucketing in sunshine to plant garden.

(more and louder crying)

Ah, but I puzzled it out and got remedy.

(getting up and indicating a spot on the floor)

Do you see the fine puddle of sunlight right here we're standing knee-deep in?

MAN, **FATHER**, **DAUGHTER.** We do.

WOMAN. Why, I mean to dismember my house – every board and nail and ratchet and blandishment of it – and relocate it right on top of the sunshine puddle, capturing it for all time.

FATHER. And that's your remedy?

WOMAN. It is. And a onerous job but I don't mind, as it's my house and I'm obliged to do right by it.

(Gestures they should lean in. They do. Speaking confidentially.)

Only this time? No door. It's the door is the trouble. Sunshine sees the way out and takes it.

(very sure of it)

I blame the door.

FATHER. *(can stand no more of this foolishness)* And here's the end of it!

(taking charge)

Have you a tool, missus?

WOMAN. *(checking apron pockets)* I got a slammer, a slicer, a bender and a boom.

FATHER. The slicer.

(WOMAN hands FATHER slicer. Goes to HOUSE.)

WOMAN. With care now. It got a cantankerous sharp edge…

(FATHER starts sawing with great vigor through one of the HOUSE's arms. Horrified.)

Ah, you're attacking the poor house!

HOUSE 1. Are you mad?

HOUSE 2. Ain't no cause!

HOUSE 3. Done nothing!

HOUSE 4. Ain't house's fault!

HOUSE 5. Don't deserve it!

HOUSE 6. You're destroying a innocent wall!

HOUSE 7. What's the poor wall done to you?

HOUSE 8. We'll be ruined to smithereens!

FATHER. *(finishes sawing)* And there it is!

WOMAN. *(completely disgusted)* House and myself likewise appalled at your crime!

FATHER. *(leads WOMAN to newly created window)* No crime's been done and have a look.

WOMAN. *(Sticks her head into the window. Leans back out to report.)* Why, sunshine is flooding in!

(Takes another look. Leans back to report.)

Under the nonces!

(Another look. Another report.)

Over the jabooms! I could go wading in the stuff!

(standing back and admiring the hole in the wall)

Does the miracle have a name?

FATHER. It does. Architectural device named window.

(handing her slicer)

Slice in two or twelve, as needed.

WOMAN. *(pocketing slicer, picking up bucket)* And will. Soon's I plant them cabbages. First things last is how it gets done, if it does and most days it don't.

(Exits left. **HOUSE** *exits after her.)*

MAN. And that's a fool or I'm a filbert.

FATHER. A greater fool in her sleep than yourself awake.

MAN. And that counts fools to two.

(happily taking **DAUGHTER***'s hand)*

FATHER. *(removing* **DAUGHTER***'s hand from* **MAN***, stepping between them)* And a last to locate.

DAUGHTER. *(Can't wait.)* And then we're wed!

MAN, FATHER, DAUGHTER. And up and off and round the town we walk, we walk, we walk…

(Walk in a circle, picking up chair and placing it center, as **BRIDE, WEDDING GUEST 1** *and* **WEDDING GUEST 2** *enter from left.* **WEDDING GUEST 1** *carries broomstick.* **WEDDING GUEST 3** *and* **WEDDING GUEST 4** *enter from right.* **BRIDE** *gets on chair and sits on the back of it.* **WEDDING GUEST 1** *and* **WEDDING GUEST 2** *stand left of chair.* **WEDDING GUEST 3** *and* **WEDDING GUEST 4** *stand right of chair.* **WEDDING GUEST 1** *and* **WEDDING GUEST 3** *hold the broomstick level with the* **BRIDE***'s head.)*

WEDDING GUESTS 3 & 4. *(yelling at* **WEDDING GUESTS 1 & 2***)* Off with her head!

WEDDING GUESTS 1 & 2. *(yelling at* **WEDDING GUESTS 3 & 4***)* Off with its legs!

WEDDING GUESTS 3 & 4. Off with her head!

WEDDING GUESTS 1 & 2. Off with its legs!

MAN. Here's a mess and I wager a fool at the foot of it.

(to **WEDDING GUEST 1***)*

Pardon, ma'am, any fools about?

WEDDING GUEST 1. *(shocked at the question)* No, sir, for they ain't allowed this side of the ocean.

WEDDING GUESTS 3 & 4. Off with her head!

WEDDING GUESTS 1 & 2. Off with its legs!

MAN. So what's the tumult?

WEDDING GUEST 1. Why, it's an attempted wedding, sir.

DAUGHTER. *(very interested)* Is it?

WEDDING GUEST 3. It is.

(indicating chair)

Do you see the donkey beast here?

MAN, FATHER, DAUGHTER. We do.

WEDDING GUEST 1. Do you see it's rid by a girl and not just any girl, but a girl bouqueted and flowered and ribboned up to a bride in veil and trainments?

MAN, FATHER, DAUGHTER. We do.

WEDDING GUEST 3. And on other side of gate, out of sight, waits wedding-to-be with groom and priest and feast.

WEDDING GUEST 1. Ah, but here's the punch. It's the rule of the world that bride riding to wedding must ride on donkey…

WEDDING GUEST 3. *(indicating broomstick)* And under this gate here a-twined with flowers.

WEDDING GUEST 1. Why, if it ain't done just so, no church nor no priest'll see them wed.

DAUGHTER. So it's tantamount.

WEDDING GUEST 3. It is.

DAUGHTER. And why the stoppage?

WEDDING GUEST 1. The bride herself to tell it.

BRIDE. *(very discouraged and weary)* Ah, miss, it's the gate ain't allowing it. For the top of the gate hangs thus. And my head is adjoined thus. And when donkey beast proceeds it's…

*(**BRIDE** hits head on broomstick.)*

ALL. Whomp!

BRIDE. *(wobbles this way and that)* And I go dizzy and got to be revived and once revived, replanted on donkey beast and re-aimed and…

*(**BRIDE** hits head on broomstick.)*

ALL. Whomp!

BRIDE. *(wobbling)* Same every time. It's turning overall tiresome. Plus, my forehead got a ache straight through to its back.

WEDDING GUEST 2. So we, bride's family, say: Off with the donkey's legs!

WEDDING GUEST 4. And we, groom's family, say: Off with the brides' head!

WEDDING GUEST 2. *(very sure of it)* We blame the donkey!

WEDDING GUEST 4. *(very sure of it)* We blame the bride!

BRIDE. *(very sure of it)* I blame the gate!

*(**BRIDE** hits head on broomstick.)*

ALL. Whomp!

*(**BRIDE** wobbles.)*

WEDDING GUEST 4. And I, speaking for groom's family and proud owner of the donkey lent today as honor to bride and occasion, say it's a delightful beast needs four legs to function.

WEDDING GUEST 2. And I, speaking for bride's family, say use of donkey appreciated but bride here is a delightful beast also, plus needs her head to function.

WEDDING GUEST 4. And it's a waste of a donkey to whoppet off its legs!

WEDDING GUEST 2. And it's a waste of a bride to whoppet off her head!

TOWN CRIER. *(enters right, ringing bell)* Hear ye, hear ye!

(stops ringing bell)

Report from wedding-to-be within:

(rings bell)

Priest's asleep!

(rings bell)

Groom's dusty!

(rings bell)

Feast's moldering!

(rings bell)

Carry on!

(Rings bell. Exits right.)

WEDDING GUESTS 3 & 4. Off with her head!

WEDDING GUESTS 1 & 2. Off with its legs!

DAUGHTER. *(can stand no more of this foolishness)* And here's the end of it!

(to BRIDE)

Miss Bride, ma'am, I'm bride-to-be myself and so can be trusted. Have you legs of your own?

BRIDE. I do.

DAUGHTER. Where do you keep them?

BRIDE. *(lifting apron, showing legs)* Here.

DAUGHTER. How many?

BRIDE. Just the two.

DAUGHTER. Do they walk?

BRIDE. They do.

DAUGHTER. Off the beast then.

BRIDE. *(Reluctant. Suspecting a trick.)* Ah. Do you mean to whoppet off my legs?

DAUGHTER. No need. Nor head neither. Take a step down.

(BRIDE gets off chair.)

And here.

(positions BRIDE next to chair)

And here.

(Places BRIDE's hand on back of chair. To WEDDING GUESTS.)

So is Bride on donkey?

WEDDING GUEST 2. Bride's hand is on donkey…

WEDDING GUEST 4. Brides's hand is part of bride…

WEDDING GUESTS 1, 2, 3, and 4

(a great revelation)

So Bride is on donkey!

DAUGHTER. So wedding is on!
WEDDING GUESTS 1, 2, 3 and 4

(very happy)

Wedding's on!

(As **WEDDING GUESTS 2 & 4** *proudly carry chair with* **BRIDE**'s *hand on it under broomstick:)*

DAUGHTER. And in you go! And all the luck!

*(***BRIDE, WEDDING GUESTS 1 & 3** *exit right.* **WEDDING GUESTS 2 & 4** *place chair center and also exit.)*

MAN. So do you reckon that crowd for a crowd of fools?

FATHER. Every neck of them topped with a head foolish as feathers.

MAN. So that counts to three fools, ripe as rain, and a handful more tossed in besides.

MAN & DAUGHTER. *(with great hope)* Wedding on?

FATHER. *(not very happy about it)* On.

MAN & DAUGHTER. *(Delighted. Clasp hands.)* On!

FATHER. *(resigned to it)* And home…

FATHER, DAUGHTER, MAN. And up and off and round the town we walk, we walk, we walk…

(Walk in a circle. **DAUGHTER** *and* **MAN** *holding hands,* **FATHER** *following begrudgingly along behind. They stop at chair.* **MAN** *and* **DAUGHTER** *stand in front of chair, facing each other and holding hands as* **PRIEST** *enters and stands on chair.)*

FATHER. And so the priest.

PRIEST. *(extending hands in a priestly gesture)* Dearly beloved all gathered. Do you?

MAN & DAUGHTER. *(happy)* We do!

PRIEST. Done. And so married. And there's the last nail in the coffin.

(Folds hands. Waits reverently.)

MAN & DAUGHTER. *(very happy)* Ah!

FATHER. *(taking **DAUGHTER** aside)* Now, Daughter, I kept my word and you're married to pieces but promise your old father that when a sweet baby floats down out of baby heaven, child's name won't be Banana Sandwich In A Boat.

DAUGHTER. *(very sure of herself)* Ah, never worry, Father. Naming of children is province of the mother and I have my own ideas about such things and I'm wife and mother and queen of the world and won't be stopped.

FATHER. *(very relieved)* Thank the firmament.

*(**DAUGHTER** and **FATHER** join **MAN** and **PRIEST**.)*

ACTOR. *(enters right carrying baby)* Year goes by, taking a year to do it.

*(Handing baby to **DAUGHTER**. Exits left.)*

MAN. *(very proud and happy)* First child!

DAUGHTER. *(admiring baby)* Startling and profound and luminescent.

MAN. *(very eager)* To be named…!

DAUGHTER. *(stopping him with an upraised hand)* Ah!

*(gestures for **PRIEST** to lean down, whispers in **PRIEST**'s ear)*

PRIEST. *(extending hands in a priestly gesture)* This child is christened before heaven and all wonderment to the name Red Shoes On A Shelf At Midnight!

(Folds hands. Waits reverently.)

FATHER. *(horrified)* Ah! There ain't no name in the name!

ACTOR. *(enters right carrying baby)* Second year goes by, trailing the first.

*(Handing baby to **DAUGHTER**. Exits left.)*

MAN. *(very proud and happy)* Second child!

DAUGHTER. *(admiring baby)* Perfect and original and dumbfounding as first.

MAN. *(very eager)* To be named…!

DAUGHTER. *(stopping him with upraised hand)* Ah!

(gestures for **PRIEST** *to lean down, whispers in* **PRIEST***'s ear)*

PRIEST. *(extending hands in priestly gesture)* This second child is christened before heaven and all wonderment and the miraculous stars to the name Whiskers In A Blue Bottle Under A Tree!

(Folds hands. Waits reverently.)

FATHER. *(more horrified)* It ain't a name! It's noise only!

ACTOR. *(enters right carrying baby)* Third year goes by following those previous, as required.

(Handing baby to **DAUGHTER***. Exits left.)*

MAN. *(very proud and happy)* Third child!

DAUGHTER. *(admiring baby)* Astounding and heart-stopping and supernatural as the rest.

MAN. *(very eager)* To be named…!

DAUGHTER. *(stopping him with upraised hand)* Ah!

(Her heart softens and she relents.)

Ah, I've had two turns so grant this third to the husband.

FATHER. *(can stand no more of this foolishness)* Never! That child will be named Banana Sandwich In A Boat over my dead body!

DAUGHTER. *(The obedient daughter. To* **MAN***.)* We must acquiesce, Husband, for he's father and boss of the world.

(to **FATHER***)*

As you say, Father.

(gestures for **PRIEST** *to lean down, whispers in* **PRIEST***'s ear)*

PRIEST. *(Extending hands in a priestly gesture.)* And this child is christened before the heavens and all wonderment and the miraculous stars and the fontons of the universe to the name Banana Sandwich In A Boat Over My Dead Body!

(Folds hands. Waits reverently.)

FATHER. *(gives up)* Ah, I shouldn't have worried about a fool marrying into the family. For there was a fool in the family from the first.

DAUGHTER. Who, Father?

FATHER. You, Daughter.

DAUGHTER. I am. For its love makes us foolish and here I am happiest of fools with all my babies smiling their gummy smiles.

FATHER. And I'd be the greatest fool of the world if I didn't love them, scurmudgeondy names and all. Hand one over.

DAUGHTER. *(handing* **FATHER** *third baby)* There she is.

FATHER. *(admiring baby)* So this is Banana Sandwich In A Boat Over My Dead Body?

DAUGHTER. It is.

ALL. *(cast enters and forms a line, all admiring the baby)* Aaaaaaaaaaaaah.

FATHER. *(very proud and pleased)* It suits her.

ALL. *(facing audience)* And it did and it does and here's the end of it!

(bow)

SAMUEL FRENCH STAFF

Nate Collins
President

Ken Dingledine
Director of Operations,
Vice President

Bruce Lazarus
Executive Director,
General Counsel

Rita Maté
Director of Finance

ACCOUNTING
- **Lori Thimsen** | Director of Licensing Compliance
- **Nehal Kumar** | Senior Accounting Associate
- **Glenn Halcomb** | Royalty Administration
- **Jessica Zheng** | Accounts Receivable
- **Andy Lian** | Accounts Payable
- **Charlie Sou** | Accounting Associate
- **Joann Mannello** | Orders Administrator

BUSINESS AFFAIRS
- **Caitlin Bartow** | Assistant to the Executive Director

CORPORATE COMMUNICATIONS
- **Abbie Van Nostrand** | Director of Corporate Communications

CUSTOMER SERVICE AND LICENSING
- **Brad Lohrenz** | Director of Licensing Development
- **Laura Lindson** | Licensing Services Manager
- **Kim Rogers** | Theatrical Specialist
- **Matthew Akers** | Theatrical Specialist
- **Ashley Byrne** | Theatrical Specialist
- **Jennifer Carter** | Theatrical Specialist
- **Annette Storckman** | Theatrical Specialist
- **Dyan Flores** | Theatrical Specialist
- **Sarah Weber** | Theatrical Specialist
- **Nicholas Dawson** | Theatrical Specialist
- **David Kimple** | Theatrical Specialist

EDITORIAL
- **Amy Rose Marsh** | Literary Manager
- **Ben Coleman** | Literary Associate

MARKETING
- **Ryan Pointer** | Marketing Manager
- **Courtney Kochuba** | Marketing Associate
- **Chris Kam** | Marketing Associate

PUBLICATIONS AND PRODUCT DEVELOPMENT
- **Joe Ferreira** | Product Development Manager
- **David Geer** | Publications Manager
- **Charlyn Brea** | Publications Associate
- **Tyler Mullen** | Publications Associate
- **Derek P. Hassler** | Musical Products Coordinator
- **Zachary Orts** | Musical Materials Coordinator

OPERATIONS
- **Casey McLain** | Operations Supervisor
- **Elizabeth Minski** | Office Coordinator, Reception
- **Coryn Carson** | Office Coordinator, Reception

SAMUEL FRENCH BOOKSHOP (LOS ANGELES)
- **Joyce Mehess** | Bookstore Manager
- **Cory DeLair** | Bookstore Buyer
- **Sonya Wallace** | Bookstore Associate
- **Tim Coultas** | Bookstore Associate
- **Alfred Contreras** | Shipping & Receiving

LONDON OFFICE
- **Anne-Marie Ashman** | Accounts Assistant
- **Felicity Barks** | Rights & Contracts Associate
- **Steve Blacker** | Bookshop Associate
- **David Bray** | Customer Services Associate
- **Robert Cooke** | Assistant Buyer
- **Stephanie Dawson** | Amateur Licensing Associate
- **Simon Ellison** | Retail Sales Manager
- **Robert Hamilton** | Amateur Licensing Associate
- **Peter Langdon** | Marketing Manager
- **Louise Mappley** | Amateur Licensing Associate
- **James Nicolau** | Despatch Associate
- **Martin Phillips** | Librarian
- **Panos Panayi** | Company Accountant
- **Zubayed Rahman** | Despatch Associate
- **Steve Sanderson** | Royalty Administration Supervisor
- **Douglas Schatz** | Acting Executive Director
- **Roger Sheppard** | I.T. Manager
- **Debbie Simmons** | Licensing Sales Team Leader
- **Peter Smith** | Amateur Licensing Associate
- **Garry Spratley** | Customer Service Manager
- **David Webster** | UK Operations Director
- **Sarah Wolf** | Rights Director

SAMUELFRENCH.COM
SAMUELFRENCH-LONDON.CO.UK

GET THE NAME OF YOUR CAST AND CREW IN PRINT WITH SPECIAL EDITIONS!

Special Editions are a unique, fun way to commemorate your production and RAISE MONEY.

The Samuel French Special Edition is a customized script personalized to *your* production. Your cast and crew list, photos from your production and special thanks will all appear in a Samuel French Acting Edition alongside the original text of the play.

These Special Editions are powerful fundraising tools that can be sold in your lobby or throughout your community in advance.

These books have autograph pages that make them perfect for year book memories, or gifts for relatives unable to attend the show. Family and friends will cherish this one of a kind souvenir.

Everyone will want a copy of these beautiful, personalized scripts!

ORDER YOUR COPIES TODAY!
E-MAIL SPECIALEDITIONS@SAMUELFRENCH.COM
OR CALL US AT 1-866-598-8449!